FOUNDATIONS A

A modified version of ExpressWays

Steven J. Molinsky · Bill Bliss

Prentice Hall, Englewood Cliffs, NJ 07632

Library of Congress Cataloging-in-Publication Data
(Revised for vol. 1)

Molinsky, Steven J.
ExpressWays : English for communication.

Includes indexes.
1. English language—Text-books for foreign speakers.
I. Bliss, Bill. II. Title.
PE1128.M674 1986 428.3′4 85-30059
ISBN 0-13-298423-7 (v. 1)

Editorial/production supervision and
interior design: Sylvia Moore
Development: Ellen Lehrburger
Cover design: Lundgren Graphics, Ltd.
Manufacturing buyer: Peter Havens
Page layout: Diane Koromhas

Illustrations and cover drawing by Gabriel Polonsky

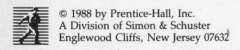

Printed in the United States of America

10 9 8 7 6 5 4 3 2

ISBN 0-13-297730-3 01

Prentice-Hall International (UK) Limited, *London*
Prentice-Hall of Australia Pty. Limited, *Sydney*
Prentice-Hall Canada Inc., *Toronto*
Prentice-Hall Hispanoamericana, S.A., *Mexico*
Prentice-Hall of India Private Limited, *New Delhi*
Prentice-Hall of Japan, Inc., *Tokyo*
Simon & Schuster Asia Pte. Ltd., *Singapore*
Editora Prentice-Hall do Brasil, Ltda., *Rio de Janeiro*

Contents

TO THE TEACHER

ExpressWays is a functional English program for adult and young-adult learners of English. The program consists of the following components:

Student Course Books—offering intensive conversational practice;
Companion Workbooks—offering grammar, reading, writing, and listening comprehension practice fully coordinated with the student course books;
Guide Books—providing background notes and expansion activities for all lessons and step-by-step instructions for teachers;
Audio Program—offering realistic presentation of dialogs in the texts;
Picture Program—including Picture Cards for vocabulary development and Dialog Visual Cards that depict scenes and characters from the texts;
Placement and Achievement Testing Program—providing tools for the evaluation of student levels and progress.

ExpressWays—Foundations is intended for adult and young-adult students of English at the very beginning level. It provides an introduction to basic grammar and vocabulary and the usage of English for everyday life situations. The text is organized by topics, or competencies, while incorporating integrated coverage of functions and beginning-level grammar.

ExpressWays—Foundations is a simplified version of *ExpressWays—Book 1*, containing shorter dialogs, easier language, and fewer exercises. It is designed for students who require more basic material and who perhaps have more limited reading and writing skills. *ExpressWays—Foundations* and *ExpressWays—Book 1* correspond to each other page for page. The texts have been designed in this way so that they may be used simultaneously in the same class with students at varying degrees of beginning-level skill.*

THE DIMENSIONS OF COMMUNICATION: FUNCTION, FORM, AND CONTENT

A number of texts present a "topical," or competency-based, syllabus by covering vocabulary items and key expressions needed for specific situations. A number of other texts present a "functional" syllabus by describing language use and listing sets of functional phrases. In both cases, texts tend to focus exclusively on the one dimension of communication that organizes the syllabus. In addition, both topical and functional texts do not usually give students intensive communicative practice using the

* For students who are non-literate, the *ExpressWays* Program offers a special readiness book that precedes *ExpressWays—Foundations. Access* builds literacy and numeracy skills while providing very basic communication practice. It offers intensive preparation for "access" to the *ExpressWays* Program.

correct grammatical forms that are required by particular key expressions or functional language choices.

ExpressWays—Foundations aims to provide dynamic, communicative practice that involves students in lively interactions based on the content of real-life contexts and situations. The topically organized syllabus is fully integrated into a complete conversational course in which students not only learn the vocabulary and expressions needed for essential life situations, but also learn the various ways to express the functions of English and intensively practice the grammatical forms required to competently produce these expressions and functions.

Every lesson in the program offers students simultaneous practice with one or more functions, the grammatical forms needed to express those functions, and the contexts and situations in which the functions and grammar are used. This "tri-dimensional clustering" of function, form, and content is the organizing principle behind each lesson and the cornerstone of the *ExpressWays* approach to functional syllabus design.

ExpressWays aims to offer students broad exposure to uses of language in a variety of relevant contexts: in community, academic, employment, home, and social settings. The characters portrayed are people of different ages, ethnic groups, and occupations, interacting in real-life situations.

While some texts make a point of giving students a range of ways of expressing a function, from extremely polite to very impolite, we have chosen to "take the middle ground" and concentrate on those expressions that would most frequently occur in normal polite conversation between people in various settings. *ExpressWays* does offer a variety of registers, from the formal language someone might use in a job interview, with a customer, or when speaking with an authority figure, to the informal language someone would use when talking with family members, co-workers, or friends.

A special feature of the program is the treatment of discourse strategies. Students actively practice initiating conversations and topics, hesitating, checking and indicating understanding, and other conversation skills.

AN OVERVIEW

Guided Conversations

Guided Conversations are the dialogs and exercises that are the central learning devices in the program. Each lesson begins with a model guided conversation that depicts a real-life situation and the vocabulary, grammar, and functions used in the communication exchange. In the exercises that follow, students create new conversations by placing new contexts, content, or characters into the framework of the model.

Interchange

This end-of-chapter activity offers students the opportunity to create and present "guided role plays." Each activity consists of a model that students can practice and then use as a basis for their original presentations. Students should be encouraged to be inventive and to use new vocabulary in these presentations and should feel free to adapt and expand the model any way they wish.

Scenes & Improvisations

These "free role plays" appear after every third chapter, offering review and synthesis of lessons in the three preceding chapters. Students are presented with eight scenes depicting conversations between people in various situations. They use the information in the scenes to determine who the people are and what they are talking about. Then, students improvise based on their perceptions of the scenes' characters, contexts, and situations.

The purpose of these improvisations is to offer free recombination practice that promotes students' absorption of the preceding chapters' vocabulary, grammar, and functions into their repertoire of active language use.

Support and Reference Sections

ExpressWays offers a number of support and reference sections:

- *Chapter Opening Pages* provide an overview of topics, grammar, and key functions and conversation strategies highlighted in each chapter.
- *End-of-Chapter Summaries* provide complete lists of topic vocabulary appearing in each chapter.
- A *Chapter-by-Chapter Grammar Summary* in the Appendix provides an overview of key grammatical structures included in each chapter.
- A *Chapter-by-Chapter Summary of Functions and Conversation Strategies* in the Appendix provides an overview of all expressions for the functions and conversation strategies in each chapter.
- A *Topic Vocabulary Glossary* provides a listing of key vocabulary domains included in the text and indicates the pages where the words first appear.
- An *Index of Functions and Conversation Strategies*, an *Index of Topics* and an *Index of Grammatical Structures* provide a convenient reference for locating coverage of functions, topics, and grammar in the text.

THE TOTAL *ExpressWays* PROGRAM

The *ExpressWays Student Course Books* are essentially designed to offer intensive communicative practice. These texts may be used independently, or in conjunction with the *ExpressWays Companion Workbooks*, which offer practice in the other skill areas of reading, writing, and listening, as well as focused practice with particular grammar structures as they occur in the program. Each exercise in the Companion Workbook indicates the specific Student Course Book page that it corresponds to.

The *ExpressWays Guide Books* provide step-by-step instructions for coverage of each lesson, background notes, sample answers to guided conversation exercises, and answer keys and listening-activity scripts for exercises in the Companion Workbooks. For teachers of multi-level classes, the Guide Books indicate for each lesson the corresponding page in *ExpressWays—Books 1* and 2 that cover the same topic.

Perhaps the most important feature of the Guide Books is the expansion exercise that is recommended for each lesson. These exercises offer students free, spontaneous practice with the vocabulary, grammar, and functions that are presented in the Student Course Books. Activities include improvisations, "information gap" role plays, problem-solving, and topics for discussion and debate. We encourage teachers to use these activities or similar ones as springboards to help their students "break away" from the text and incorporate lesson content into their everyday use of English.

The *ExpressWays Audio Program* includes a set of tapes providing realistic presentation of all model dialogs and selected guided conversation exercises in the Student Course Books. The tapes are designed to be used interactively, so that the recorded voice serves as the student's speaking partner, making conversation practice possible even when the student is studying alone. The Audio Program also includes a set of tapes for the listening comprehension exercises in the Companion Workbooks.

The *ExpressWays Picture Program* includes Dialog Visual Cards and Picture Cards. The *ExpressWays Dialog Visual Cards* are poster-size illustrations depicting the characters and settings of all model dialogs. Their use during introduction of the model helps to assure that students are engaged in active listening and speaking practice during this important stage in the lesson. The *ExpressWays Picture Cards* illustrate key concepts and vocabulary items. They can be used for introduction of new material, for review, for enrichment exercises, and for role-playing activities.

The *ExpressWays Testing Program* includes a Placement Testing Kit for initial evaluation and leveling of students, and sets of Mid-Term and Final Examinations to measure students' achievement at each level of the program. All tests in the program include both oral and written evaluation components.

SUGGESTED TEACHING STRATEGIES

In using *ExpressWays,* we encourage you to develop approaches and strategies that are compatible with your own teaching style and the needs and abilities of your students. While the program does not require any specific method or technique in order to be used effectively, you may find it helpful to review and try out some of the following suggestions. (Specific step-by-step instructions may be found in the Guide Books.)

Guided Conversations

1. *Setting the Scene.* Have students look at the model illustration in the book or on the *ExpressWays* Dialog Visual Card. Set the scene: Who are the people? What is the situation?
2. *Listening to the Model.* With books closed, have students listen to the model conversation—presented by you, a pair of students, or on the audio tape.
3. *Class Practice.* With books still closed, model each line and have the whole class repeat in unison.
4. *Reading.* With books open, have students follow along as two students present the model.

   (At this point, ask students if they have any questions and check understanding of new vocabulary. You may also want to call students' attention to any related language or culture notes, which can be found in the Guide Book.)
5. *Pair Practice.* In pairs, have students practice the model conversation.
6. *Exercise Practice.* (optional) Have pairs of students simultaneously practice all the exercises.
7. *Exercise Presentations.* Call on pairs of students to present the exercises.

   (At this point, you may want to discuss any language or culture notes related to the exercises, as indicated in the Guide Book.)

Expansion

We encourage you to use the expansion activity for each lesson suggested in the Guide Book or a similar activity that provides students with free, spontaneous practice while synthesizing the content of the lesson.

Interchange

Have students practice the model using the same steps listed above for guided conversations. (You might want to eliminate the *Class Practice* step in the case of longer Interchange dialogs.) After practicing the model, have pairs of students create and present original conversations using the model dialog as a guide. Encourage students to be inventive and to use new vocabulary. (You may want to assign this exercise as homework, having students prepare their own conversations, practice them the next day with another student, and then present them to the class.) Students should present their conversations without referring to the written text, but they should also not memorize them. Rather, they should feel free to adapt and expand them any way they wish.

Scenes & Improvisations

Have students talk about the people and the situations, and then present role plays based on the scenes. Students may refer back to previous lessons as a resource, but they should not simply re-use specific conversations. (You may want to assign these exercises as written homework, having students prepare their conversations, practice them the next day with another student, and then present them to the class.)

Multi-Level Classes

Teachers of multi-level classes may consider using *ExpressWays—Foundations* and *ExpressWays—Book 1* simultaneously. Since the texts follow the same topical curriculum and essentially cover the same material page for page, they may be used in the same class with students at varying degrees of beginning-level skill. Teachers may choose to present the model dialogs from either of the texts and then have students practice in pairs or small groups using the particular text they have been assigned. During such pair or group work, the teacher may wish to offer special help to students using *ExpressWays—Foundations*, while allowing students using *ExpressWays—Book 1* to work more independently, or it may be desirable to pair students at different levels so that a student using *Book 1* provides assistance to a student using the *Foundations* book.

In conclusion, we have attempted to offer students a communicative, meaningful, and lively way of practicing the vocabulary, grammar, and functions of English. While conveying to you the substance of our textbook, we hope that we have also conveyed the spirit: that learning to communicate in English can be genuinely interactive . . . truly relevant to our students' lives . . . and fun!

Steven J. Molinsky
Bill Bliss

Components of an ExpressWays Lesson

A **model conversation** offers initial practice with the functions and structures of the lesson.

Does This Bus Go to Westville?

A. Excuse me. Does this bus go to Westville?
B. No, it doesn't. It goes to Riverside.
A. Which bus goes to Westville?
B. The Number 30 bus.
A. Thanks.

1. train
the "D" train

2. plane
flight 64

3. train
the "Capitol Express"

4. bus
Bus Number 27

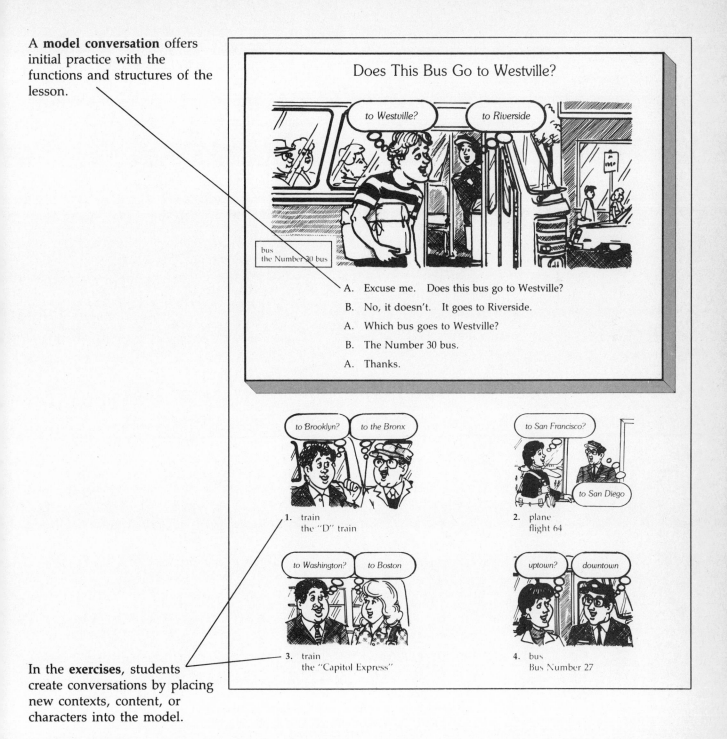

In the **exercises**, students create conversations by placing new contexts, content, or characters into the model.

Examples:

Exercise 1:

A. Excuse me. Does this train go to Brooklyn?
B. No, it doesn't. It goes to the Bronx.
A. Which train goes to Brooklyn?
B. The "D" Train.
A. Thanks.

Exercise 2:

A. Excuse me. Does this plane go to San Francisco?
B. No, it doesn't. It goes to San Diego.
A. Which plane goes to San Francisco?
B. Flight 64.
A. Thanks.

- **PERSONAL INFORMATION**
- **SOCIAL COMMUNICATION**

- **To Be** • **WH-Questions**

1

Hello
Let Me Introduce . . .
What's Your Last Name?
What's Your Address?
Where Are You From?
Nice to Meet You

- Greeting People • Introductions
- Asking for and Reporting Information

Hello

A. Hello. My name is Carlos.

B. Hi. I'm Kim. Nice to meet you.

A. Nice meeting you, too.

1.

2.

3.

4.

Let Me Introduce . . .

husband

A. Hi! How are you?

B. Fine. And you?

A. Fine, thanks. Let me introduce my husband.

B. Nice to meet you.

1. wife

2. father

3. mother

4. brother

What's Your Last Name?

A. What's your last name?

B. Sanchez.

A. Could you spell that, please?

B. S-A-N-C-H-E-Z.

A. And your first name?

B. Maria.

1. John Clayton

2. Nancy Brenner

3. Linda Kwan

4. Robert Kelton

What's Your Address?

10 Main Street
423-6978

A. What's your address?

B. 10 Main Street.

A. And your telephone number?

B. 423-6978.

1. 5 Summer Street
531-7624

2. 7 Pond Road
899-3263

3. 14 Maple Avenue
475-1182

4. 19 Howard Road
542-7306*

* 0 = "oh"

Where Are You From?

A. What's your name?

B. Kenji.

A. Where are you from?

B. Japan.

1. Maria
Italy

2. Hector
Mexico

3. Mohammed
Egypt

4. Anna
The Soviet Union

INTERCHANGE
Nice to Meet You

A. Hello. My name is Franco Rossi.

B. Hello. I'm Harry Miller.

A. Where are you from?

B. New York. How about you?

A. I'm from Rome.

B. Nice to meet you.

A. Nice meeting you, too.

Franco Rossi Rome	Harry Miller New York

1. Carol Williams — Toronto | Carmen Lopez — Mexico City

2. Charles Whitmore — London | Ali Hassan — Cairo

3. David Clarke — Melbourne | Asako Tanaka — Tokyo

4. Rick Starlight — Hollywood | Natasha Markova — Moscow

You're an airplane passenger. Create an original conversation.

CHAPTER 1 TOPIC VOCABULARY

Personal Information

name
last name
first name
address
street
road
avenue
telephone number

Family Members

husband
wife
father
mother
brother

Countries

Egypt
Italy
Japan
Mexico
The Soviet Union

• TELEPHONE • GETTING AROUND TOWN
• SOCIAL COMMUNICATION

• Subject Pronouns • To Be: Am/Is/Are
• To Be: Yes/No Questions
• To Be: Negative Sentences
• Present Continuous Tense • Possessive Adjectives
• WH-Questions

2

I'd Like the Number of Mary Nielson
I'm Sorry. You Have the Wrong Number
Is Peter There?
Where Are You Going?
What Are You Doing?
I Can't Talk Right Now. I'm Taking a Shower

• Asking for and Reporting Information • Greeting People
• Identifying • Leave Taking

I'd Like the Number of Mary Nielson

863-4227

A. What city?

B. Chicago. I'd like the number of Mary Nielson.

A. What street?

B. Hudson Avenue.

A. Just a moment . . . The number is 863-4227.

1. 968-3135

2. 747-6360

3. 237-8044

4. 328-1191

I'm Sorry. You Have the Wrong Number

A. Hello.

B. Hello, Fred?

A. I'm sorry. You have the wrong number.

B. Is this 328-7178?

A. No, it isn't.

B. Oh. Sorry.

1.

2.

3.

4.

Is Peter There?

A. Hello. Is Peter there?

B. No. He's at the supermarket.

A. Oh. I'll call back later. Thank you.

A. Hello. Is Janet there?

B. No. She's at the bank.

A. Oh. I'll call back later. Thank you.

A. Hello. Are Timmy and Billy there?

B. No. They're at the library.

A. Oh. I'll call back later. Thank you.

1.

2.

3.

4.

Where Are You Going?

A. Where are you going?

B. To the library. How about you?

A. I'm going to the post office.

B. Well, nice seeing you.

A. Nice seeing you, too.

1.

2.

3.

4.

What Are You Doing?

A. What are you doing?

B. I'm fixing my car.

A. What's Linda doing?

B. She's studying.

A. What's John doing?

B. He's cleaning the garage.

A. What are you doing?

B. We're doing our homework.

1. Richard
fixing his bicycle

2. you
making breakfast

3. Jennifer and Melissa
cleaning their room

4. Kevin
dancing

INTERCHANGE
I Can't Talk Right Now. I'm Taking a Shower

A. Hello, Steve? This is Jackie.
B. Hi. Listen, I can't talk right now.
   I'm taking a shower.
A. Oh, okay. I'll call back later.
B. Speak to you soon.
A. Good-bye.

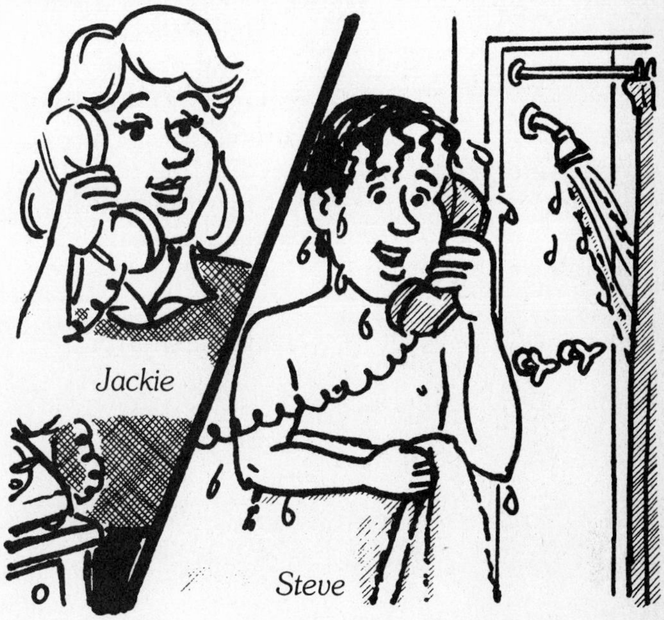

taking a shower

1. studying

2. eating lunch

3. cooking dinner

4. feeding the baby

A friend is calling you on the telephone, but you can't talk right now. Create an original conversation.

CHAPTER 2 TOPIC VOCABULARY

Community	Everyday Activities	Telephone	Family Members
bank	cleaning (my) room	number	baby
clinic	cleaning the garage		parents
laundromat	cooking dinner		
library	doing (my) homework		
mall	eating lunch		
movies (movie theater)	feeding the baby		
museum	fixing (my) bicycle		
park	fixing (my) car		
post office	making breakfast		
school	studying		
supermarket	taking a shower		

• GETTING AROUND TOWN
• TRANSPORTATION

3

• There Is • Prepositions of Location
• Simple Present Tense
• Simple Present Tense vs. To Be • Short Answers
• Imperatives • WH-Questions

Is There a Post Office Nearby?
Does This Bus Go to Westville?
Is This Bus Number 42?
How Do I Get to the Bus Station?
Can You Tell Me How to Get to the Museum?
Can You Tell Me How to Get to Franklin's Department Store?
Excuse Me. I'm Lost

• Directions–Location • Asking for and Reporting Information
• Attracting Attention • Gratitude
• Checking and Indicating Understanding • Asking for Repetition

Is There a Post Office Nearby?

A. Excuse me. Is there a post office nearby?

B. Yes. There's a post office on Main Street.

A. On Main Street?

B. Yes. It's next to the bank.

A. Thank you.

A. Excuse me. Is there a laundromat nearby?

B. Yes. There's a laundromat on Grand Avenue.

A. On Grand Avenue?

B. Yes. It's across from the bus station.

A. Thank you.

A. Excuse me. Is there a drug store nearby?

B. Yes. There's a drug store on River Street.

A. On River Street?

B. Yes. It's between the library and the clinic.

A. Thank you.

A. Excuse me. Is there a supermarket nearby?

B. Yes. There's a supermarket on Davis Boulevard.

A. On Davis Boulevard?

B. Yes. It's around the corner from the movie theater.

A. Thank you.

1. hotel?

2. parking lot?

3. grocery store?

4. gas station?

5. park?

6. clinic?

Does This Bus Go to Westville?

bus
the Number 30 bus

A. Excuse me. Does this bus go to Westville?

B. No, it doesn't. It goes to Riverside.

A. Which bus goes to Westville?

B. The Number 30 bus.

A. Thanks.

1. train
the "D" train

2. plane
flight 64

3. train
the "Capitol Express"

4. bus
Bus Number 27

Is This Bus Number 42?

A. Is this Bus Number 42?

B. Yes, it is.

A. Oh, good! I'm on the right bus!

A. Is this the "F" train?

B. No, it isn't.

A. Oops! I'm on the wrong train!

A. Does this bus stop at Center Street?

B. Yes, it does.

A. Oh, good! I'm on the right bus!

A. Does this plane go to Florida?

B. No, it doesn't.

A. Oops! I'm on the wrong plane!

1.

2.

3.

4.

How Do I Get to the Bus Station?

A. Excuse me. How do I get to the bus station?

B. Walk THAT way. The bus station is on the left, next to the post office.

A. Thank you.

1.

2.

3.

4.

Can You Tell Me How to Get to the Museum?

A. Excuse me. Can you tell me how to get to the museum?

B. Yes. Walk to Second Avenue and turn right.

A. Uh-húh.

B. Then, walk two blocks to Grove Street.

A. Okay.

B. Then, turn left on Grove Street and look for the museum on the right.

A. Thank you very much.

1.

2.

3.

Can You Tell Me How to Get to Franklin's Department Store?

A. Excuse me. Can you tell me how to get to Franklin's Department Store?

B. Sure. Take the Second Avenue bus and get off at Park Street.

A. I'm sorry. Did you say the Second Avenue bus?

B. Yes. That's right.

A. Thanks very much.

1.

2.

3.

4.

Excuse Me. I'm Lost

A. Excuse me. I'm lost. Can you tell me how to get to the Holiday Hotel?

B. Sure. Drive that way two miles. Then, take the expressway to Exit 14. Okay so far?

A. Yes.

B. Then, turn right and look for the Holiday Hotel on the left. Have you got that?

A. Yes. Thanks very much.

A. Excuse me. I'm lost. Can you tell me how to get to ____________________?

B. Sure. ____.
Then, ______________________________________. Okay so far?

A. Yes.

B. Then, ____.
Have you got that?

A. Yes. Thanks very much.

You're lost! Ask for directions.

CHAPTER 3 TOPIC VOCABULARY

Community

bank
bus station
clinic
department store
drug store
gas station
grocery store
hospital
hotel
laundromat
library
movie theater
museum
park
parking lot
police station
post office
shopping mall
supermarket
theater
train station

Transportation

bus
plane
train

expressway
exit

SCENES & IMPROVISATIONS
Chapters 1, 2, 3

Who are these people?
What are they saying?

1.

2.

3.

4.

5.

6.

7.

8.

• HOUSING • FOOD
• SUPERMARKET

• Singular/Plural • Count/Non-Count Nouns
• This/That/These/Those • There Is/There Are
• Articles: A/An • Article: The
• Imperatives • Have/Has
• Simple Present Tense vs. To Be

4

We're Looking for a Two-Bedroom Apartment
Is There a Refrigerator in the Kitchen?
How Much Is the Rent?
Where Do You Want This Sofa?
There Aren't Any More Cookies
There Isn't Any More Milk
Excuse Me. Where Are the Carrots?
Mmm! This Cake Is Delicious!

• Asking for and Reporting Information • Want–Desire
• Hesitating • Checking and Indicating Understanding

We're Looking for a Two-Bedroom Apartment

A. We're looking for a two-bedroom apartment.

B. I think I have an apartment for you. It has two bedrooms, a large living room, and a very nice kitchen.

1. a three-bedroom apartment

2. a one-bedroom apartment

3. a two-bedroom apartment

4. a one-bedroom apartment

Is There a Refrigerator in the Kitchen?

A. Is there a refrigerator in the kitchen?

B. Yes, there is.

A. And how many windows are there in the living room?

B. There are four windows in the living room.

1.

2.

3.

4.

How Much Is the Rent?

A. How much is the rent?

B. $700 a month plus electricity.

A. $700 a month plus electricity?

B. That's right. Do you want to see the apartment?

A. Yes.

1.

2.

3.

4.

Where Do You Want This Sofa?

A. Where do you want this sofa?

B. That sofa? Hmm. Please put it in the living room.

A. And how about these chairs?

B. Those chairs? Let me see. Please put them in the dining room.

1.

2.

3.

4.

There Aren't Any More Cookies

A. What are you looking for?

B. A cookie.

A. I'm afraid there aren't any more cookies.

B. Oh.

1.

2.

3.

4.

There Isn't Any More Milk

A. What are you looking for?

B. Milk.

A. I'm afraid there isn't any more milk.

B. Oh.

1.

2.

3.

4.

Excuse Me. Where Are the Carrots?

A. Excuse me. Where are the carrots?

B. They're in Aisle J.

A. I'm sorry. Did you say "A"?

B. No. "J."

A. Oh. Thank you.

A. Excuse me. Where's the butter?

B. It's in Aisle 3.

A. I'm sorry. Did you say "C"?

B. No. "3."

A. Oh. Thanks.

1.

2.

3.

4.

INTERCHANGE
Mmm! This Cake Is Delicious!

A. Mmm! This cake is delicious! What's in it?

B. Let me think . . . some eggs, some sugar, some flour, and some raisins.

A. It's excellent!

B. I'm glad you like it.

A. Mmm! These egg rolls are delicious! What's in them?

B. Let me think . . . some cabbage, some pork, some shrimp, and some bean sprouts.

A. They're excellent!

B. I'm glad you like them.

You're eating at your friend's home. The food is delicious. Compliment your friend.

CHAPTER 4 TOPIC VOCABULARY

Housing

bathroom
bedroom
dining room
kitchen
living room
patio

cabinet
closet
fireplace
refrigerator
shower
stove
window

apartment
building
elevator
floor

electricity
gas
heat
rent

Furniture

bed
chair
crib
lamp
picture
plant
rug
sofa
table
TV

Foods

apple
banana
bean sprouts
bread
butter
cabbage
cake
carrot
cheese
cookie
egg
egg rolls
flour
ice cream
lettuce
milk
peach
pork
potato
raisins
rice
shrimp
sugar
tomato
yogurt

• EMPLOYMENT/GETTING A JOB
• PERSONAL INFORMATION • MONEY

• Can • Simple Present Tense
• Time Expressions • To Be
• Past Tense: Preview • May

5

What Job Do You Have Open?
Can I Come In for an Interview?
I'm a Very Experienced Sales Clerk
I Can Learn Quickly
Are You Currently Employed?
What Does a Stock Clerk Do Here?
Can You Tell Me About the Work Schedule and the Salary?
Tell Me a Little More About Yourself

• Asking for and Reporting Information
• Asking for and Reporting Additional Information
• Ability/Inability • Certainty/Uncertainty
• Checking and Indicating Understanding • Hesitating

What Job Do You Have Open?

A. What job do you have open?
B. We're looking for a cook.
A. I'd like to apply.
B. Can you make eggs and sandwiches?
A. Yes, I can.
B. Okay. Here's an application form.
A. Thank you.

make eggs and sandwiches?

1. fix cars?

2. clean rooms and make beds?

3. use a cash register?

4. operate kitchen equipment?

Can I Come In for an Interview?

A. I'm calling about your ad for a secretary.

B. I see. Can you type?

A. Yes, I can. Can I come in for an interview?

B. Yes. What's your name?

A. Ann Kramer.

B. Can you come in on Monday at 10:00?*

A. On Monday at 10:00? Yes. Thanks very much.

1. Tuesday
   2:00

2. Wednesday
   3:00

3. Thursday
   1:30†

4. Friday
   9:30

* 10:00 = ten o'clock † 1:30 = one thirty

I'm a Very Experienced Sales Clerk

A. I'm a very experienced sales clerk.

B. Tell me about your skills.

A. I can talk with customers and I can use a cash register.

B. Can you take inventory?

A. Yes. I can take inventory very well.

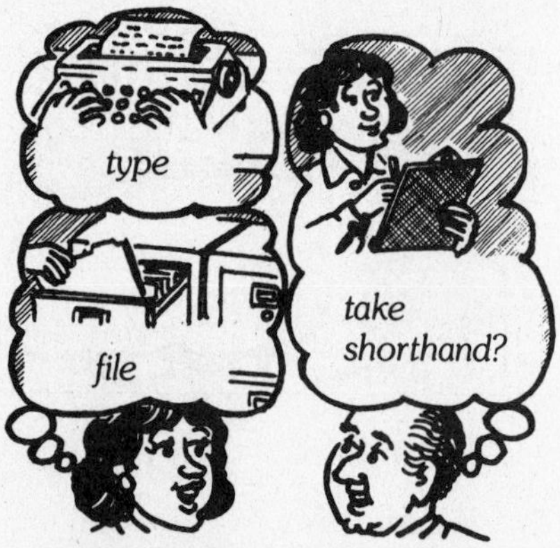

1. secretary

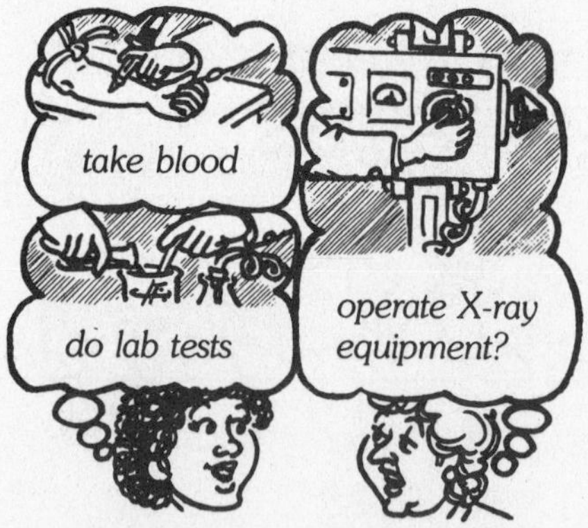

2. medical technician

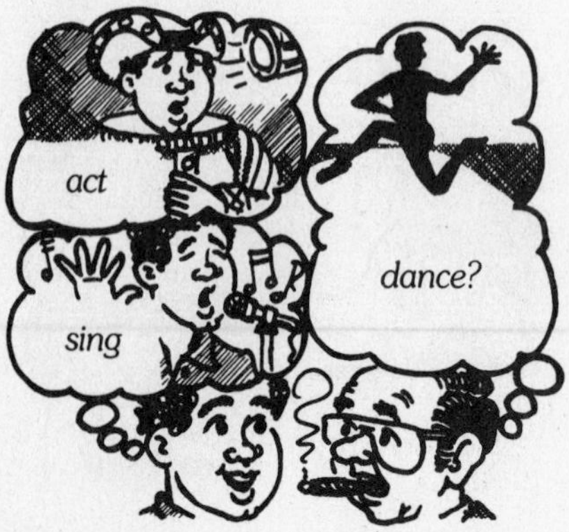

3. actor

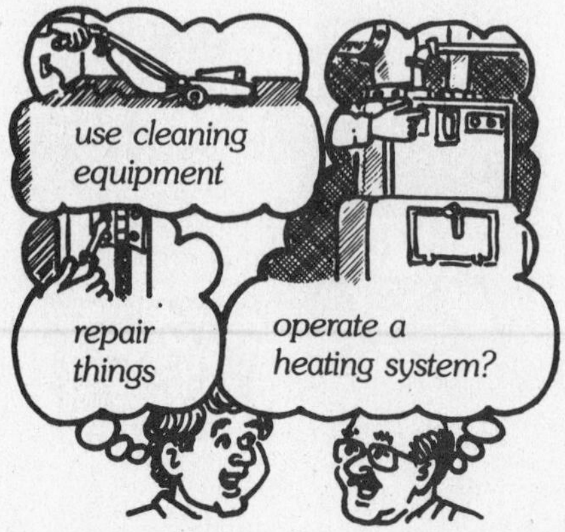

4. custodian

I Can Learn Quickly

A. Can you use a copying machine?

B. No, I can't. But I can learn quickly.

A. Are you sure?

B. Yes. I'm positive.

1.

2.

3.

4.

Are You Currently Employed?

yes
Tyler's Department Store
3 years

no
the Seven Seas Restaurant
1 year

A. Are you currently employed?

B. Yes, I am. I work at Tyler's Department Store.

A. And what is your position?

B. I'm a salesperson.

A. How long have you worked there?

B. Three years.

A. Are you currently employed?

B. No, I'm not. My last job was at the Seven Seas Restaurant.

A. And what was your position?

B. I was a waiter.

A. How long did you work there?

B. One year.

1. yes
the Crown Insurance Company
2 years

2. no
the Broadway Coffee Shop
9 months

3. no
the Adult Learning Center
5 years

4. yes
the Ajax Security Company
7 months

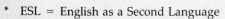

* ESL = English as a Second Language

What Does a Stock Clerk Do Here?

A. What does a stock clerk do here?

B. A stock clerk stocks the shelves and cleans the aisles. Can you do that?

A. Yes, definitely! I stock the shelves and clean the aisles in my present job.

1. a housekeeper

2. a waiter

3. a salesperson

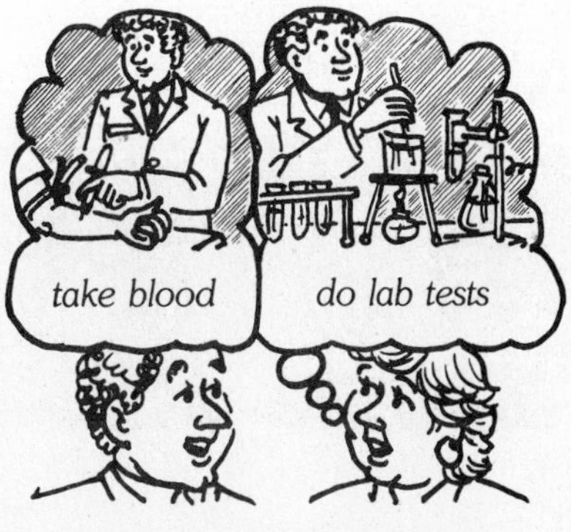

4. a medical technician

Can You Tell Me About the Work Schedule and the Salary?

A. Can you tell me about the work schedule?

B. Yes. Hours are from nine (9:00)* to five thirty (5:30).

A. I see. And may I ask about the salary?

B. Yes. The salary is five dollars ($5.00) an hour.

1.

2.

3.

4.

* 9:00 = "nine o'clock" or "nine"
1:00 = "one o'clock" or "one"

INTERCHANGE
Tell Me a Little More About Yourself

A. Tell me a little more about yourself.

B. All right. Let's see . . . I'm married. My husband's name is Richard. He's a security guard at the National Motors factory. We have two children, a son and a daughter.

A. Do you have any hobbies or special interests?

B. Yes. I play the piano and I take dance lessons.

A. I see. Tell me, do YOU have any questions for ME?

B. No, I don't think so. Thank you for your time.

A. My pleasure. You'll hear from us soon.

A. Tell me a little more about yourself. B. All right. Let's see . . . ____________. A. Do you have any hobbies or special interests? B. Yes. I ____________. A. I see. Tell me, do YOU have any questions for ME? B. No, I don't think so. Thank you for your time. A. My pleasure. You'll hear from us soon.

You're at a job interview. Create an original conversation.

CHAPTER 5 TOPIC VOCABULARY

Occupations

actor
cashier
cook
custodian
dishwasher
driver
ESL teacher
housekeeper
lab technician
mechanic
medical technician
office assistant
sales clerk
salesperson
science teacher
secretary
security guard
stock clerk
typist
waiter
waitress

Job Skills

act
clean *rooms*
clean *the aisles*
dance
do *lab tests*
drive *a truck*
file
fix *cars*
help *customers*
make *beds*
make *eggs and sandwiches*
make *salads*
operate *a forklift*
operate *a heating system*
operate *kitchen equipment*
operate *office equipment*
operate *X-ray equipment*
repair *things*
repair *vacuum cleaners and toasters*
serve *the food*
sing
stock *the shelves*
take *blood*
take *inventory*
take *orders*
take *shorthand*
talk *with customers*
teach *Biology*
type
use *a cash register*
use *a copying machine*
use *cleaning equipment*
use *laboratory equipment*
use *word-processing equipment*

Family Members

children
daughter
husband
son

Getting a Job

ad
application form
employed
experienced
hobbies
hours
interview
job
position
salary
skills
special interests
work schedule

Days of the Week

Sunday
Monday
Tuesday
Wednesday
Thursday
Friday
Saturday

Time

hour
day
week
month
year

• HEALTH • DRUG STORE
• EMERGENCIES

• Imperatives • Have • Can • Should
• Simple Present Tense vs. To Be
• Present Continuous Tense • Short Answers
• Time Expressions
• Prepositions of Location • Count/Non-Count Nouns

6

I Have a Headache
What Do You Recommend?
I'd Like to Make an Appointment
Do You Smoke?
Touch Your Toes
You Should Go on a Diet
Take One Tablet Three Times a Day
I Want to Report an Emergency!

• Asking for and Reporting Information • Instructing
• Advice–Suggestions • Directions–Location
• Checking and Indicating Understanding
• Initiating a Topic

I Have a Headache

A. You don't look very well.
Are you feeling okay?

B. Not really. I have a headache.

A. I'm sorry to hear that.

1.

2.

3.

4.

What Do You Recommend?

A. Excuse me. Can you help me?
B. Yes.
A. I have a bad cold. What do you recommend?
B. I recommend Maxi-Fed Cold Medicine.
A. Oh. Where can I find it?
B. It's in Aisle 2.
A. Thank you.

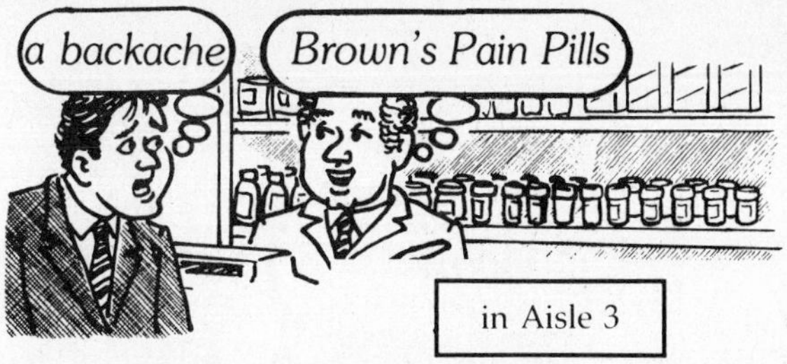

A. Excuse me. Can you help me?
B. Yes.
A. I have a backache. What do you recommend?
B. I recommend Brown's Pain Pills.
A. Oh. Where can I find them?
B. They're in Aisle 3.
A. Thank you.

1. in Aisle 1

2. in Aisle 4

3. in Aisle 2 on the right

4. in Aisle 5 on the left

I'd Like to Make an Appointment

A. Doctor's Office.

B. Hello. This is John Stevens. I'd like to make an appointment.

A. What's the problem?

B. My right foot hurts very badly.

A. Can you come in tomorrow morning at 9:15?*

B. Tomorrow morning at 9:15? Yes. Thank you.

1. Karen Fuller

2. Sally Wilson

3. Mr. Beck

4. Ms. Wong

* 9:15 = nine fifteen
† 11:45 = eleven forty-five

Do You Smoke?

A. One more question.

B. All right.

A. Do you smoke?

B. No, I don't.

A. Okay. That's all the information I need. The doctor will see you shortly.

B. Thank you.

1.

2.

3.

4.

Touch Your Toes

A. Touch your toes.
B. My toes?
A. Yes.

A. Take off your shirt.
B. My shirt?
A. Yes.

A. Sit on the table.
B. On the table?
A. Yes.

A. Hold your breath.
B. Hold my breath?
A. Yes.

1.

2.

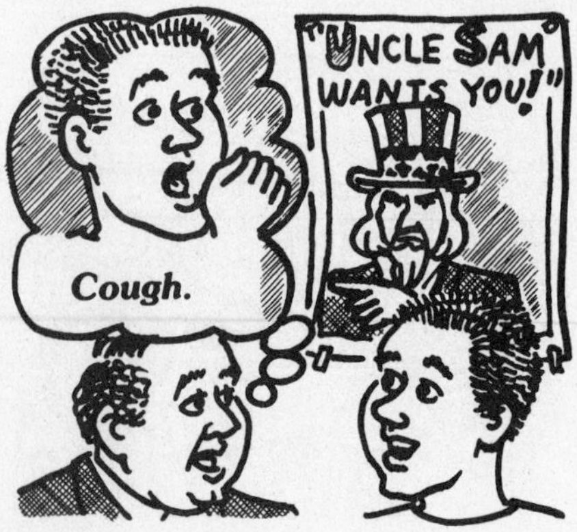

3.

4.

You Should Go on a Diet

weight
go on a diet

A. I'm concerned about your weight.

B. My weight?

A. Yes. You should go on a diet.

B. I see.

1. lungs
   stop smoking

2. back
   exercise daily

3. blood pressure
   change your diet

4. gums
   use dental floss

Take One Tablet Three Times a Day

A. Here's your medicine.

B. Thank you.

A. Be sure to follow the directions.
Take one tablet three times a day.

B. I understand. One tablet three times a day.

A. That's right.

1.

2.

3.

4.

I Want to Report an Emergency!

A. Police.

B. I want to report an emergency!

A. Yes?

B. I think my father is having a heart attack!

A. What's your name?

B. Diane Perkins.

A. And the address?

B. 76 Lake Street.

A. Telephone number?

B. 293-7637.

A. All right. We'll be there right away.

B. Thank you.

Diane Perkins
76 Lake Street
293-7637

1. Neal Stockman
193 Davis Avenue
458-9313

2. Janet Brown
17 Park Road
963-2475

3. Carol Weaver
1440 Lexington Boulevard
354-6260

4. Henry Stewart
5 Linden Lane
723-0980

You're reporting an emergency. Create an original conversation.

CHAPTER 6 TOPIC VOCABULARY

Health

allergies
backache
bleeding
choking
cold
cough
dizzy
earache
headache
heart attack
heart disease
sore throat
stiff neck
stomachache
toothache

back
ear
foot
gums
lungs
neck
toes

blood pressure
diet
weight

Medicine

aspirin
cold medicine
cough syrup
ear drops
pain pills
penicillin

capsule
pill
tablet
teaspoon

Emergencies

ambulance
emergency
fire department
hospital
police
police emergency unit

Personal Information

name
address
telephone number

Family Members

daughter
father
son
wife

SCENES & IMPROVISATIONS
Chapters 4, 5, 6

Who are these people?
What are they saying?

1.

2.

3.

4.

5.

6.

7.

8.

7

• CLOTHING • DEPARTMENT STORE
• MONEY • POST OFFICE

• Singular/Plural • Prepositions of Location
• Adjectives • Too + Adjective
• Ordinal Numbers • Want to
• Question Formation

I'm Looking for a Shirt
May I Help You?
It's Too Short
Excuse Me. Where Are the Rest Rooms?
I'd Like to Buy This Watch
I Want to Return This Fan
I Want to Buy Some Stamps, Please
I'd Like to Mail This Package to Detroit

• Want–Desire • Directions–Location
• Satisfaction/Dissatisfaction
• Attracting Attention • Gratitude
• Checking and Indicating Understanding
• Hesitating

I'm Looking for a Shirt

A. Excuse me. I'm looking for a shirt.

B. Shirts are in Aisle 3.

A. Thank you.

A. Excuse me. I'm looking for a tie.

B. Ties are on that counter.

A. Thank you.

A. Excuse me. I'm looking for a dress.

B. Dresses are over there.

A. Thank you.

A. Excuse me. I'm looking for a pair of pants.

B. Pants are on that rack.

A. Thank you.

1.

2.

3.

4.

May I Help You?

A. May I help you?

B. Yes, please. I'm looking for a belt.

A. What size?

B. Size 36.

A. And what color?

B. Black.

A. Okay. Let's see . . . a size 36 black belt. Here you are.

B. Thank you very much.

1.

2.

3.

4.

* $15\frac{1}{2}$ = fifteen and a half

It's Too Short

A. How does the jacket fit?
B. It's too short.
A. Here. I think this jacket will fit better.
B. Thanks very much.

A. How do the pants fit?
B. They're too long.
A. Here. I think these pants will fit better.
B. Thanks very much.

1. skirt

2. sneakers

3. blouse

4. gloves

Excuse Me. Where Are the Rest Rooms?

A. Excuse me. Where are the rest rooms?

B. They're on the fourth floor.

A. The fourth floor?

B. Yes.

A. Thanks.

A. Excuse me. Where's the elevator?

B. It's in the back of the store.

A. The back of the store?

B. Yes.

A. Thanks.

1.

2.

3.

4.

I'd Like to Buy This Watch

A. I'd like to buy this watch.

B. Okay. That's twenty-six ninety-five ($26.95).

A. Excuse me, but I don't think that's the right price.

B. Oh. You're right. It's on sale. That'll be twenty-five dollars and forty-seven cents ($25.47).

A. I'd like to buy these earrings.

B. Okay. That's twelve fifty ($12.50).

A. Excuse me, but I don't think that's the right price.

B. Oh. You're right. They're on sale. That'll be six dollars and fifty-six cents ($6.56).

1. necklace

2. boots

3. camera

4. stockings

I Want to Return This Fan

A. I want to return this fan.
B. What's the matter with it?
A. It's too noisy.
B. Do you have the receipt?
A. Yes. Here you are.

A. I want to return these jeans.
B. What's the matter with them?
A. They're too short.
B. Do you have the receipt?
A. Yes. Here you are.

1. purse
small

2. pajamas
tight

3. coat
heavy

4. videogames
easy

I Want to Buy Some Stamps, Please

A. I want to buy some stamps, please.

B. You can buy stamps at Window Number 2.

A. Window Number 2?

B. Yes.

A. Thank you.

1. mail a package

2. buy a money order

3. send a registered letter

4. buy an aerogramme

INTERCHANGE
I'd Like to Mail This Package to Detroit

A. I'd like to mail this package to Detroit.

B. How do you want to send it?

A. First class, please.

B. Do you want to insure it?

A. Hmm. I don't know.

B. Well, is it valuable?

A. Yes. It's a camera. Please insure it for fifty dollars ($50).

B. All right. That's four dollars and thirty-seven cents ($4.37), please.

A. I'd like to mail this package to ________.

B. How do you want to send it?

A. First class, please.

B. Do you want to insure it?

A. Hmm. I don't know.

B. Well, is it valuable?

A. Yes. It's a ________. Please insure it for ________ dollars.

B. All right. That's ________ dollars and ________ cents, please.

You're mailing a package at the post office. Create an original conversation.

CHAPTER 7 TOPIC VOCABULARY

Clothing

belt
blouse
coat
dress
jacket
necklace
purse
raincoat
shirt
skirt
sweater
tie
umbrella
watch

boots
earrings
gloves
jeans
pajamas
pants
shoes
sneakers
stockings

Department Store

aisle
counter
dressing room
elevator
price
rack
receipt
rest rooms
sale
table

bedroom furniture
camera
fan
radio
refrigerator
TV
videogame

Colors

black
brown
gray
green
yellow

Describing

big
easy
heavy
large
long
noisy
short
small
tight

Post Office

aerogramme
money order
package
registered letter
stamps

first class
insure
window

• EMPLOYMENT/ON THE JOB

• Past Tense • Imperatives • Object Pronouns
• Time Expressions • Can • Could
• Adjectives • Prepositions of Location
• Singular/Plural

8

Excuse Me. Where's the Supply Room?
Please Take This Box to Mr. Miller on the 3rd Floor
Can You Show Me How to Turn On This Machine?
Can You Tell Me How to Transfer a Call?
Could You Show Me How?
Did I Wash the Glasses All Right?
Did I Type the Letters All Right?
You Must Wear Your Helmet at All Times
I'm Free Now. What Do You Want Me to Do?

• Requests • Instructing • Attracting Attention
• Approval/Disapproval • Apologizing
• Checking and Indicating Understanding
• Asking for Repetition
• Focusing Attention

Excuse Me. Where's the Supply Room?

A. Excuse me. Where's the supply room?
B. It's down the hall.
A. Thank you.

1.

2.

3.

4.

Please Take This Box to Mr. Miller on the 3rd Floor

He's tall, with brown hair.

A. Please take this box to Mr. Miller on the 3rd floor.

B. I'm sorry, but I'm new here. What does he look like?

A. He's tall, with brown hair.

B. Okay. I'll do it right away.

1. She's short, with blonde hair.

2. He's very tall and thin.

3. He's heavy, with curly dark hair.

4. She's average height, with gray hair.

Can You Show Me How to Turn On This Machine?

turn on this machine

A. Excuse me. Can you help me for a minute?

B. Sure. What is it?

A. Can you show me how to turn on this machine?

B. Yes. Press this button.

A. I see. Thanks very much.

B. You're welcome.

1. turn off this light

2. open this door

3. start this dishwasher

4. punch in

Can You Tell Me How to Transfer a Call?

A. Excuse me. Can you tell me how to transfer a call?

B. Yes. Press the red button. Then, dial the other office and hang up.

A. I see. First, I press the red button. Then, I dial the other office and hang up. Right?

B. Yes. That's right.

A. Thank you.

B. You're welcome.

transfer a call

1. use the postage machine

2. light this oven

3. operate the freight elevator

4. fill out this timesheet

Could You Show Me How?

Take out your tray.
Close the drawer.
Turn the key on the side.

lock the cash register

A. How's your first day on the job going?

B. Fine.

A. Tell me, do you know how to lock the cash register?

B. No. Could you show me how?

A. All right. First, take out your tray. Then, close the drawer.

B. I'm sorry. Could you please repeat that?

A. Sure. First, take out your tray.

B. Um-hmm.

A. Then, close the drawer. Okay so far?

B. Yes. I'm following you.

A. Then, turn the key on the side. Have you got that?

B. Yes. I understand. Thank you.

A. How's your first day on the job going?

B. Fine.

A. Tell me, do you know how to ________________________________?

B. No. Could you show me how?

A. All right. First, ________________________________.
Then, ________________________________.

B. I'm sorry. Could you please repeat that?

A. Sure. First, ________________________________.

B. Um-hmm.

A. Then, ________________________________. Okay so far?

B. Yes, I'm following you.

A. Then, ________________________________. Have you got that?

B. Yes. I understand. Thank you.

Place the paper on the glass.
Put down the cover.
Press the start button.

1. use the copying machine

Spray the wax on the floor.
WAX
Flip this switch.
ON
OFF
Go back and forth like this.

2. use the floor polishing machine

Did I Wash the Glasses All Right?

A. Did I wash the glasses all right?
B. Yes. You washed them very well.

A. Did I clean the supply room all right?
B. Yes. You cleaned it very well.

A. Did I paint the ceiling all right?
B. Yes. You painted it very well.

A. Did I make the beds all right?
B. Yes. You made them very well.

1. stock–stocked

2. play–played

3. operate–operated

4. write–wrote

Did I Type the Letters All Right?

type–typed

A. Did I type the letters all right?

B. Actually, you typed them rather poorly.

A. Oh. I'm sorry.

B. Don't worry about it. You're new on the job.

1. cook–cooked

2. inspect–inspected

3. set–set

4. repair–repaired

You Must Wear Your Helmet at All Times

A. Johnson?

B. Yes, sir?*

A. Where's your helmet?

B. I'm afraid I left† it in my car.

A. You know, you must wear your helmet at all times.

B. I'm sorry. I forgot.†

1.

2.

3.

4.

* sir (to a man)
ma'am (to a woman)

† leave–left
forget–forgot

INTERCHANGE

I'm Free Now. What Do You Want Me to Do?

A. I'm free now. What do you want me to do?

B. Please clean the kitchen shelves.

A. I cleaned them already.

B. Oh, good. Then please sweep the floor.

A. I swept* it a little while ago. Is there anything else I can do?

B. Hmm. I don't know.

A. Do you want me to set the tables for tomorrow?

B. Yes. That's a good idea.

A. I'm free now. What do you want me to do?

B. Please ____________________.

A. I ____________________ already.

B. Oh, good. Then please ____________________.

A. I ____________________ a little while ago.
Is there anything else I can do?

B. Hmm. I don't know.

A. Do you want me to ____________________?

B. Yes. That's a good idea.

You're on the job and you're free now. Create an original conversation.

* sweep–swept

CHAPTER 8 TOPIC VOCABULARY

Places on the Job

basement
bathroom
cafeteria
employee lounge
hall
Personnel Office
supply room

Protective Clothing

gloves
hairnet
helmet
lab coat
safety glasses

Job Procedures

clean *the supply room*
close *the drawer*
cook *the eggs*
dial *the other office*
fill out *this timesheet*
flip *this switch*
hang up
inspect *the car*
light *this oven*
list *your hours*
lock *the cash register*
make *the beds*
open *this door*
operate *the freight elevator*
paint *the ceiling*
place *the paper on the glass*
press *this button*
pull *this chain*
punch in
push *this button*
put *a match in the hole*
put down *the cover*
put in *your time card*
repair *the TV*
set *the amount*
sign *at the bottom*
spray *the wax*
start *this dishwasher*
stock *the shelves*
sweep *the floor*
take out *your tray*
transfer *a call*
turn *the key*
turn off *this light*
turn on *the gas*
type *the letters*
use *the postage machine*
wash *the glasses*
write *the reports*

Objects on the Job

cash register
copying machine
floor
forklift
freight elevator
key
locker
machine
postage machine
soda machine
time card
timesheet

Describing People

height
very tall
tall
short
very short

weight
thin
heavy

hair
curly
dark
blond/blonde
brown
gray

• RECREATION
• SOCIAL COMMUNICATION
• EMPLOYMENT/ON THE JOB • WEATHER

• Past Tense • WH-Questions • Future: Going to
• Want to • Like • Like to
• Can • Have to • Time Expressions

9

What Do You Want to Do Today?
Do You Want to Play Tennis Today?
Do You Want to Get Together Tomorrow?
I'm Afraid I Can't. I Have to Work Late
What Are You Going to Do This Weekend?
How Was Your Weekend?
What Movie Did You See?
What Do You Like to Do in Your Free Time?
What Kind of Movies Do You Like?

• Want–Desire • Asking for and Reporting Information
• Invitations • Likes/Dislikes • Intention
• Obligation • Checking and Indicating Understanding

What Do You Want to Do Today?

It's raining.

A. What do you want to do today?

B. I don't know. What's the weather like?

A. It's raining. Do you want to see a movie?

B. Sure.

1. It's snowing.

2. It's sunny.

3. It's cloudy.

4. It's hot.

Do You Want to Play Tennis Today?

play–played

A. Do you want to play tennis today?

B. Not really. We played tennis last weekend.

A. Okay. What do you want to do?

B. I want to go jogging.

A. All right. That sounds like fun.

1. go–went

2. have–had

3. play–played

4. go–went

Do You Want to Get Together Tomorrow?

A. Do you want to get together tomorrow?

B. Sure. What do you want to do?

A. I don't know. What's the weather forecast?

B. It's going to be hot.

A. Oh. Let's go to the beach.

B. Okay. That sounds like fun.

1. be sunny

2. rain

3. be cold

4. snow

I'm Afraid I Can't. I Have to Work Late

A. Do you want to go out for dinner tonight?

B. Tonight? I'm afraid I can't. I have to work late.

A. That's too bad.

B. Maybe some other time.

1.

2.

3.

4.

What Are You Going to Do This Weekend?

A. What are you going to do this weekend?

B. I'm going to paint my apartment. How about you?

A. I'm going to work in my garden.

B. Well, have a good weekend!

A. You, too.

1.

2.

3.

4.

How Was Your Weekend?

A. Tell me, how was your weekend?

B. It was very nice. I went skiing. How was YOUR weekend?

A. It was okay. I stayed home and watched TV.

1.

2.

3.

4.

* read–read
take–took

What Movie Did You See?

What movie did you see?
"Dancing in the Park"

at the movies

A. I called you yesterday evening, but you weren't home.

B. I was at the movies.

A. Oh. What movie did you see?

B. I saw "Dancing in the Park."

A. Did you enjoy it?

B. Yes. It was excellent.

Who did you hear*?
the Philadelphia Orchestra

1. at the concert hall

What play did you see?
"The Friendly Garden"

2. at the theater

What did you have?
moussaka

3. at the Greek restaurant

What game did you see?
the Yankees against the Red Sox

4. at the baseball stadium

* hear–heard

What Do You Like to Do in Your Free Time?

A. Tell me, what do you like to do in your free time?

B. I like to run.

A. Oh. That's interesting. Where do you like to run?

B. In the park.

1. What . . .?

2. Where . . .?

3. What . . .?

4. What kind of books . . .?

INTERCHANGE
What Kind of Movies Do You Like?

What kind of movies* do you like?*

movie star

* comedies
westerns
dramas
mysteries
adventure movies
science fiction movies
•
•
•

A. Tell me, what kind of movies do you like?*

B. I like comedies. How about you?

A. I don't like comedies very much. I like adventure movies.

B. Oh, I see.

A. Who's your favorite movie star?

B. Eddie Murphy. How about you?

A. Harrison Ford.

A. Tell me, ______________________________?

B. I like ______________________. How about you?

A. I don't like ______________ very much. I like ______________.

B. Oh, I see.

A. Who's your favorite ______________________?

B. ______________________. How about you?

A. ______________________.

You're taking a break at work. Talk with a co-worker about music, TV, and sports.

1. What kind of music do you like?*

   singer

2. Which TV program do you like the best?*

   TV star

3. What sport* do you like the most?*

   player

* classical music
rock music
folk music
jazz
.
.
.

* "Dallas"
"Love Boat"
"Wide World of Sports"
.
.
.

* baseball
soccer
football
basketball
hockey
.
.
.

CHAPTER 9 TOPIC VOCABULARY

Weather

cloudy
cold
hot
rain
snow
sunny

Sports

baseball
basketball
football
golf
hockey
jogging
sailing
skating
skiing
soccer
swimming
tennis

Recreation and Entertainment

ballgame
baseball stadium
beach
bike ride
concert
concert hall
dancing
dinner
garden
lake
movie (the movies)
museum
park
party
picnic
play
restaurant
theater
TV
walk
zoo

Movies

adventure movies
comedies
dramas
mysteries
science fiction movies
westerns

Music

classical music
folk music
jazz
rock music

Performers

movie star
player
singer
TV star

Family Members

aunt
daughter
grandchildren
grandfather
grandmother
son
uncle
wife

SCENES & IMPROVISATIONS
Chapters 7, 8, 9

Who are these people?
What are they saying?

1.

2.

3.

4.

JOE
AL

5.

EMPLOYEES MUST

6.

MOVIES
Two Hearts
BEST RESTAURANTS IN TOWN

7.

HOT
Coffee

8.

CHAPTER-BY-CHAPTER GRAMMAR SUMMARY

CHAPTER 1

To Be

I'm from Rome.

My name **is** Carlos.
I'm Kim.

Where **are** you from?

WH-Questions

What's your name?
Where are you from?

Cardinal Numbers: 1–19

1	one	11	eleven
2	two	12	twelve
3	three	13	thirteen
4	four	14	fourteen
5	five	15	fifteen
6	six	16	sixteen
7	seven	17	seventeen
8	eight	18	eighteen
9	nine	19	nineteen
10	ten		

CHAPTER 2

Subject Pronouns

I	**I'm** sorry.
he	**He's** at the supermarket.
she	**She's** at the bank.
it	No, **it** isn't.
we	**We're** doing our homework.
you	Where are **you** going?
they	**They're** at the library.

To Be: Am/Is/Are

I **am**	**I'm** going to the post office.
he **is**	**Is** Peter there?
she **is**	**Is** Janet there?
it **is**	**Is** this 328-7178?
we **are**	**We're** doing our homework.
you **are**	Where **are** you going?
they **are**	**Are** Timmy and Billy there?

To Be: Yes/No Questions

Is this 328-7178?
Are Timmy and Billy there?

To Be: Negative Sentences

No, it **isn't**.

Present Continuous Tense

What **is** he **doing**?
What **is** she **doing**?
What **are** you **doing**?
What **are** they **doing**?

I'm fixing my car.
He's cleaning the garage.
She's studying.
We're doing our homework.
They're cleaning their room.

Possessive Adjectives

my	I'm fixing **my** car.
his	He's fixing **his** bicycle.
her	She's fixing **her** bicycle.
our	We're doing **our** homework.
your	What's **your** name?
their	They're cleaning **their** room.

WH-Questions

What are you doing?
Where are you going?

CHAPTER 3

There Is

Is there a post office nearby?
There's a post office on Main Street.

Prepositions of Location

There's a post office **on** Main Street.
It's **next to** the bank.
It's **across from** the bus station.
It's **between** the library and the clinic.
It's **around the corner from** the movie theater.

Simple Present Tense

Does this bus **go** to Westville?
No, it **doesn't**.

It **goes** to Riverside.

Simple Present Tense vs. To Be

Is this Bus Number 42?
Yes, it **is**.
No, it **isn't**.

Does this bus stop at Center Street?
Yes, it **does**.
No, it **doesn't**.

Short Answers

Yes, it is.
No, it isn't.

Yes, it does.
No, it doesn't.

Imperatives

Walk to Second Avenue and turn right.

WH-Questions

Which bus goes to Westville?

Cardinal Numbers: 20–99

20	twenty	40	forty
21	twenty-one	50	fifty
22	twenty-two	60	sixty
23	twenty-three	70	seventy
.	.	80	eighty
.	.	90	ninety
29	twenty-nine	99	ninety-nine
30	thirty		

Ordinal Numbers: 1st–5th

1st	first
2nd	second
3rd	third
4th	fourth
5th	fifth

CHAPTER 4

Singular/Plural

It has one bedroom.
It has two bedroom**s**.

Is there a refrigerator?
There are four windows.

That sofa? Put **it** in the living room.
Those chairs? Put **them** in the dining room.

Where are the carrots? /s/
potatoes? /z/
peaches? /ɪz/

Count/Non-Count Nouns

Count

There aren't any more cookies.
tomatoes.
apples.

Where are the carrots?
potatoes?
peaches?

These egg rolls **are** delicious!

Non-Count

There isn't any more milk.
bread.
cheese.

Where's the butter?
sugar?
rice?

This cake **is** delicious.

This/That/These/Those

Where do you want **this** sofa?
That sofa?
How about **these** chairs?
Those chairs?

There Is/There Are

Is there a refrigerator?
Yes, **there is**.

How many windows **are there**?
There are four windows.

There isn't any more milk.
There aren't any more cookies.

Articles: A/An

A cookie.	**An** apple.
A tomato.	**An** egg.

Article: The

Where are **the** carrots?
Where's **the** butter?

Imperatives

Please put them in the dining room.

Have/Has

I **have** an apartment for you.
It **has** two bedrooms.

Simple Present Tense vs. To Be

How much **is** the rent?

Do you want to see the apartment?

Cardinal Numbers: 100–999

100	one hundred
200	two hundred
300	three hundred
.	.
.	.
900	nine hundred
999	nine hundred (and) ninety-nine

CHAPTER 5

Can

Can you make eggs and sandwiches?
Yes, I **can**.
No, I **can't**.

I **can** use a cash register.

Can you tell me about the work schedule?

Simple Present Tense

	/s/
I	stock the shelves.
A stock clerk	stock**s** the shelves.
	/z/
I	clean rooms.
A housekeeper	clean**s** rooms.
	/ɪz/
I	use a cash register.
A salesperson	use**s** a cash register.

Do you have any hobbies?

May

May I ask about the salary?

Time Expressions

1:00	one o'clock (one)
2:00	two o'clock (two)
3:00	three o'clock (three)
.	.
.	.
12:00	twelve o'clock (twelve)
1:30	one thirty
2:30	two thirty
3:30	three thirty
.	.
.	.
12:30	twelve thirty

On Monday **at** 10:00.

Hours are **from** 9:00 **to** 5:30.

The salary is	$5.00	**an hour.**
	$250	**a week.**
	$50	**a day.**
	$15,000	**a year.**

To Be

Are you currently employed?
Yes, I **am**.
What **is** your position?
I'm a salesperson.

am	**I'm** married.
is	My husband's name **is** Richard.
	He's a security guard.

Past Tense: Preview

My last job **was** at the Seven Seas Restaurant.

What **was** your position?
I **was** a waiter.

How long **did** you work there?
One year.

Cardinal Numbers: 1,000–1,000,000

1,000	one thousand
2,000	two thousand
3,000	three thousand
.	.
.	.
10,000	ten thousand
100,000	one hundred thousand
1,000,000	one million

CHAPTER 6

Imperatives

Touch your toes.
Be sure to follow the directions.

Have

I **have** a headache.

Can

Can you help me?

Should

You **should** go on a diet.

Simple Present Tense vs. To Be

Do you smoke?
No, I **don't**.

Are you allergic to penicillin?
No, **I'm not**.
Is there a history of heart disease in your family?
No, there **isn't**.

Present Continuous Tense

My son **is feeling** very dizzy.
My ears **are ringing**.

Short Answers

No, I don't.
No, I'm not.

No, there isn't.

Time Expressions

1:15	one fifteen
2:15	two fifteen
3:15	three fifteen
.	.
.	.
12:15	twelve fifteen
1:45	one forty-five
2:45	two forty-five
3:45	three forty-five
.	.
.	.
12:45	twelve forty-five

this morning
this afternoon
tomorrow morning
tomorrow afternoon
next Monday

tomorrow morning **at** 9:15

Take one tablet three **times a day**.
twice a day.
before each meal.
after each meal.

Prepositions of Location

It's **in** Aisle 2 **on** the right.

Count/Non-Count Nouns

Count

I recommend Brown's Pain Pills.
Where can I find **them**?
They're in Aisle 3.

Non-Count

I recommend Maxi-Fed Cold Medicine.
Where can I find **it**?
It's in Aisle 2.

CHAPTER 7

Singular/Plural

/s/

I'm looking for **a shirt**.
Shirts are in Aisle 3.

/z/

I'm looking for **a tie**.
Ties are in Aisle 3.

/ɪz/

I'm looking for **a dress**.
Dresses are in Aisle 3.

I'm looking for **a pair of** pants.
a pair of shoes.

I'd like to buy **this** watch.
I'd like to buy **these** earrings.

How does the jacket fit?
It's too long.
I think **this** jacket will fit better.

How do the pants fit?
They're too long.
I think **these** pants will fit better.

Where**'s** the elevator?
Where **are** the rest rooms?

Prepositions of Location

Shirts are **in** Aisle 3.
on that counter.
in the back of the store.
in the front of the store.
near the elevator.
over there.

Adjectives

A **size 36 black** belt.
A **medium green** sweater.
A **small brown** raincoat.

It's too **short**.

Too + Adjective

It's **too short**.
They're **too long**.

Ordinal Numbers

1st first
2nd second
3rd third
4th fourth

Want To

I **want to** return this fan.

Do you **want to** insure it?
How do you **want to** send it?

Question Formation

Is it valuable?

Do you want to insure it?
How do you want to send it?

CHAPTER 8

Past Tense

/t/

You wash**ed** them very well.

/d/

You clean**ed** it very well.

/ɪd/

You paint**ed** it very well.

Did I wash the glasses all right?

make-made

Did I **make** the beds all right?
You **made** them very well.

write-wrote

Did I **write** the reports all right?
You **wrote** them very well.

set-set

Did I **set** the table all right?
You **set** it rather poorly.

leave-left

I **left** it in my car.

forget-forgot

I **forgot.**

sweep-swept

Please **sweep** the floor.
I **swept** it a little while ago.

Imperatives

Please take this box to Mr. Miller.

Press this button.

Object Pronouns

You cleaned **it** very well.
You washed **them** very well.

Can

Can you help me for a minute?

Could

Could you show me how?

Adjectives

He's **tall**, with **brown** hair.
He's **heavy**, with **curly dark** hair.

Prepositions of Location

It's **down** the hall.
It's **in** the basement.
It's **on** the left.

Singular/Plural

Where**'s** your helmet?
Where **are** your gloves?

Must

You **must** wear your helmet at all times.

CHAPTER 9

Past Tense

How **was** your weekend?
It **was** very nice.

You **weren't** home.

What movie **did** you see?
Did you enjoy it?

We play**ed** tennis last weekend.

go-went

We **went** swimming.

have-had

We **had** a picnic.

read-read

I **read** a book.

take-took

I **took** my daughter to a ballgame.

see-saw

I **saw** "Dancing in the Park."

hear-heard

I **heard** the Philadelphia Orchestra.

WH-Questions

Who did you hear?
What movie did you see?
Where do you like to swim?
What kind of books do you like to read?
How was your weekend?
Which program do you like?

Future: Going To

It's **going to** be hot.

What are you **going to** do this weekend?
I'm **going to** paint my apartment.

Want To

I **want to** go jogging.

What do you **want to** do today?
Do you **want to** see a movie?

Like To

I **like to** run.

What do you **like to** do?
Where do you **like to** run?

Like To vs. Like

What do you **like to** do?
I **like to** run.

What kind of movies do you **like**?
I **like** comedies.
I **don't like** comedies.

Can

I'm afraid I **can't**.

Have To

I **have to** work late.

Time Expressions

Do you want to go dancing
tonight?
tomorrow?
tomorrow night?
this Saturday night?
this Sunday afternoon?
this weekend?

CHAPTER-BY-CHAPTER SUMMARY OF FUNCTIONS AND CONVERSATION STRATEGIES

CHAPTER 1

Functions

Greeting People

Hello.
Hi. [less formal]

Nice to meet you.
  Nice meeting you, too.

How are you?
  Fine.
  Fine, thanks.

Introductions

Introducing Oneself

My name is *Carlos*.
I'm *Kim*.

Introducing Others

Let me introduce *my husband*.

Asking for and Reporting Information

What's your name?
What's your last name?
And your first name?

Could you spell that, please?
  S-A-N-C-H-E-Z.

What's your address?
  10 Main Street.
And your telephone number?
  423-6978.

Where are you from?
  New York.
  I'm from *New York*.

How about you?
And you?

CHAPTER 2

Functions

Asking for and Reporting Information

What city?
  Chicago.
What street?
  Hudson Avenue.

The number is *863-4227*.

Is this *328-7178?*

Is *Peter* there?
  No. *He's at the supermarket*.

Where are you going?
  To *the library*.
  I'm going to *the library*.

How about you?

What are you doing?
  I'm *fixing my car*.

Greeting People

Hello.
Hi. [less formal]

Hello, *Fred?*
Hello, *Steve?* This is *Jackie*.

Identifying

This is *Jackie*.

Leave Taking

Nice seeing you.
  Nice seeing you, too.

I'll call back later.

Speak to you soon.

Good-bye.

Apologizing

I'm sorry.
Sorry.

Gratitude

Expressing . . .

Thank you.

CHAPTER 3

Functions

Directions-Location

Asking for Directions

How do I get to ________?
Can you tell me how to get to ________?

Giving Directions

Walk THAT way.

Turn right.
Turn left.

Walk to *Second Avenue* and turn *right*.

Walk *two* blocks to *Grove Street*.

Turn *left* on *Grove Street*.

Look for the *museum* on the *right*.

Take *the Second Avenue bus* and get off at *Park Street*.
Take *the expressway* to *Exit 14*.

Drive that way *two* miles.

Inquiring about Location

Is there a *post office* nearby?

Giving Location

There's a *post office* on *Main Street*.

It's { next to / across from / around the corner from } *the bank*.
It's between *the library* and *the clinic*.

The *bus station* is { on the left. / on the right. }

The *bus station* is on the *left*, *next to the post office*.

Asking for and Reporting Information

Does this *bus* go to *Westville?*
  It goes to *Riverside*.

Which *bus* goes to *Westville?*
  The Number 30 bus.

Is this *Bus Number 42?*
Is this the *plane* to *Atlanta?*
Does this *bus* stop *at Center Street?*
Does this *plane* go to *Florida?*

Attracting Attention

Excuse me.

Gratitude

Expressing . . .

Thank you.
Thank you very much.
Thanks.
Thanks very much.

Conversation Strategies

Checking and Indicating Understanding

Checking Another Person's Understanding

Okay so far?

Have you got that?

Checking One's Own Understanding

On Main Street?

I'm sorry. Did you say *the Second Avenue bus?*

Indicating Understanding

Okay.

Uh-húh.

CHAPTER 4

Functions

Asking for and Reporting Information

Is there *a refrigerator in the kitchen?*

How many *windows* are there?

There are *four windows in the living room.*

How much is *the rent?*
$700 a month plus electricity.

There isn't any more *milk.*
There aren't any more *cookies.*

What's in it?
What's in them?

Want-Desire

Inquiring about . . .

Do you want to *see the apartment?*

Where do you want *this sofa?*

Expressing . . .

We're looking for *a two-bedroom apartment.*

Directions-Location

Inquiring about Location

Where's *the butter?*
Where are *the carrots?*

Giving Location

It's in Aisle *3.*
They're in Aisle *J.*

Describing

It has *two bedrooms.*

Instructing

Please put it *in the living room.*

Attracting Attention

Excuse me.

Correcting

Giving Correction

No. *"J."*

Gratitude

Thank you.
Thanks.

Complimenting

Expressing Compliments

Mmm!

This *cake* is delicious!
These *egg rolls* are delicious!

It's excellent!
They're excellent!

Responding to Compliments

I'm glad you like it.
I'm glad you like them.

Conversation Strategies

Hesitating

Hmm.
Let me see.
Let me think . . .

Checking and Indicating Understanding

Checking One's Own Understanding

$700 a month plus electricity?

I'm sorry. Did you say *"A?"*

CHAPTER 5

Functions

Asking for and Reporting Information

What's your name?
Ann Kramer.

Tell me about *your skills.*
Can you tell me about *the work schedule?*

What job do you have open?

Are you currently employed?
Yes, I am. I work at *Tyler's Department Store.*
No, I'm not. My last job was at *the Seven Seas Restaurant.*

What is your position?
I'm a *salesperson.*
What was your position?
I was a *waiter.*

How long have you worked there?
How long did you work there?
Three years.

What does a *stock clerk* do *here?*
A stock clerk stocks the shelves.

I *stock the shelves* in my present job.

Hours are *from nine to five thirty.*
The salary is *five dollars an hour.*

I'm *married.*

My *husband's* name is *Richard.*
He's a security guard at the National Motors factory.

We have *two* children, *a son and a daughter.*

Do you have any hobbies or special interests?
I *play the piano.*

Asking for and Reporting Additional Information

Tell me a little more about *yourself.*

And may I ask *about the salary?*

Ability/Inability

Inquiring about . . .

Can you *make eggs and sandwiches?*
Can you *come in on Monday at 10:00?*

Can you *do that?*

Expressing Ability

Yes.
Yes, I can.

I can *use a cash register.*
I can *take inventory* very well.

I can *learn quickly.*

Expressing Inability

No, I can't.

Certainty/Uncertainty

Inquiring about . . .

Are you sure?

Expressing Certainty

I'm positive.

Yes, definitely!

Requests

Direct, Polite

Can I *come in for an interview?*

Want-Desire

Expressing . . .

We're looking for *a cook.*

I'd like to *apply*.

Gratitude

Expressing . . .

Thank you.
Thanks very much.

Thank you for *your time*.

Responding to . . .

My pleasure.

Conversation Strategies

Checking and Indicating Understanding

Checking One's Own Understanding

On Monday at 10:00?

Indicating Understanding

I see.

Hesitating

Let's see . . .

CHAPTER 6

Functions

Asking for and Reporting Information

Are you feeling okay?
  Not really.

What's the problem?
  I have *a headache*.
  My *right foot* hurts very badly.
  My *neck* is very *stiff*.
  My son is feeling very *dizzy*.
  My daughter has a bad *toothache*.
  My *ears* are *ringing*.

My *father* is *having a heart attack!*
My *wife* can't *breathe!*
My *son* is *bleeding* very badly!
My apartment is on fire!
There's a *burglar in my house!*

Do you *smoke?*
Are you *allergic to penicillin?*
Is there a history of *heart disease* in your family?
Do you have *any allergies?*

I want to report an emergency!

What's your name?
  Diane Perkins.
And the address?
  76 Lake Street.
Telephone number?
  293-7637.

Instructing

Touch *your toes*.
Take off *your shirt*.
Sit *on the table*.
Hold *your breath*.
Lie *on your back*.
Look *at the ceiling*.

Be sure to *follow the directions*.

Take *one tablet three times* a day.
Take *two tablets* before *each meal*.
Take *two capsules* after *each meal*.

Advice-Suggestions

Asking for . . .

What do you recommend?

Offering . . .

I recommend *Maxi-Fed Cold Medicine*.

You should *go on a diet*.

Directions-Location

Inquiring about Location

Where can I find *it?*
Where can I find *them?*

Giving Location

It's in Aisle 2.

It's in Aisle 2 { on the right. / on the left. }

Sympathizing

I'm sorry to hear that.

Attracting Attention

Excuse me.

Requests

Direct, Polite

Can you help me?

Gratitude

Expressing . . .

Thank you.

Identifying

Doctor's Office.
Police.
City Hospital.
Jones Ambulance Company.
Fire Department.
Police Emergency Unit.

Want-Desire

Expressing . . .

I'd like to *make an appointment*.

Ability/Inability

Inquiring about . . .

Can you *come in tomorrow morning?*

Asking for and Reporting Additional Information

One more question.

Fear-Worry-Anxiety

I'm concerned about *your weight*.

Conversation Strategies

Checking and Indicating Understanding

Checking One's Own Understanding

Tomorrow morning at 9:15?
My toes?
My weight?

One tablet three times a day.

Indicating Understanding

I see.
I understand.

CHAPTER 7

Functions

Want-Desire

Inquiring about . . .

How do you want to *send it?*

Expressing . . .

I'm looking for *a shirt*.

I'd like to *buy this watch*.
I want to *return this fan*.
I want to *buy some stamps*, please.

Directions-Location

Inquiring about Location

Where are *the rest rooms?*

Giving Location

Shirts are {
in Aisle 3.
over there.
on that *counter*.
in the back of *the store*.
in the front of *the store*.
on the *fourth* floor.
near *the elevator*. }

Satisfaction/Dissatisfaction

Inquiring about . . .

How *does the jacket fit?*

Expressing Dissatisfaction

It's too *short*.
They're too *long*.

Attracting Attention

Excuse me.

Gratitude

Expressing . . .

Thank you.
Thank you very much.
Thanks.
Thanks very much.

Requests

Direct, Polite

Please *insure it for fifty dollars*.

Responding to Requests

All right.

Offering to Help

Making an Offer

May I help you?

Responding to an Offer

Yes, please.

Asking for and Reporting Information

That's *twenty-six ninety-five*.
That'll be *twenty-six ninety-five*.

It's *on sale*.
They're *on sale*.

What's the matter with *it*?

Is it *valuable?*
Yes. It's a *camera*.

Correcting

Giving Correction

Excuse me, but I don't think *that's the right price*.

Responding to Correction

Oh. You're right.

Conversation Strategies

Checking and Indicating Understanding

Checking One's Own Understanding

Okay. Let's see . . . *a size 36 black belt*.

The fourth floor?
Window Number 2?

Hesitating

Hmm.

CHAPTER 8

Functions

Requests

Direct, Polite

Please *take this box to Mr. Miller*.

Can you *show me how to turn on this machine?*

Direct, More Polite

Can you help me for a minute?

Could you *show me how?*

Responding to Requests

Yes.
Sure.
All right.

Instructing

Press *this button*.
Pull *this chain*.
Push *this button*.
Flip *this switch*.

Put in your time card like this.

First, *take out your tray*.
Then, *close the drawer*.

Attracting Attention

Excuse me.

Johnson?

Approval/Disapproval

Inquiring about . . .

Did I *wash the glasses* all right?

Expressing Approval

You *washed them* very well.

Expressing Disapproval

You *typed them* rather poorly.

Apologizing

I'm sorry.

I'm sorry, but *I'm new here*.

Directions-Location

Inquiring about Location

Where's *the supply room?*

Giving Location

It's down the hall.
It's down the hall on the *left*.
It's in the *basement*.
It's the *first* door on the *right*.

Gratitude

Expressing . . .

Thank you.
Thanks very much.

Responding to . . .

You're welcome.

Asking for and Reporting Information

What does he look like?

How's *your first day on the job going?*
Fine.

Tell me, ________?

Where's *your helmet?*

Describing

He's *tall*, with *brown* hair.

Ability/Inability

Inquiring about . . .

Do you know how to *lock the cash register?*

Granting Forgiveness

Don't worry about it.

Denying/Admitting

Admitting

I'm afraid *I left it in my car*.

Remembering/Forgetting

Indicating . . .

I forgot.

Offering to Help

Making an Offer

I'm free now. What do you want me to do?

Is there anything else I can do?

Do you want me to *set the tables?*

Obligation

Expressing . . .

You must *wear your helmet at all times*.

Conversation Strategies

Checking and Indicating Understanding

Checking Another Person's Understanding

Okay so far?

Have you got that?

Checking One's Own Understanding

First, *I press the button*. Then, *I dial the office*. Right?

Indicating Understanding

I see.

Yes. That's right.

Um-hmm.

I'm following you.
I understand.

Asking for Repetition

I'm sorry. Could you please repeat that?

Focusing Attention

You know, *you must wear your helmet*.

Hesitating

Hmm.

CHAPTER 9

Functions

Want-Desire

Inquiring about . . .

What do you want to do?
What do you want to do today?

Do you want to *see a movie?*

Expressing . . .

I want to *go jogging*.

Asking for and Reporting Information

Tell me, ________?

What's the weather like?
It's *raining*.

What's the weather forecast?
It's going to *be hot*.

How was *your weekend?*
It was *very nice*.

I was at *the movies*.

What *movie* did you *see?*
Who did you *hear?*

Invitations

Extending . . .

Do you want to *get together tomorrow?*

Accepting . . .

Sure.

That sounds like fun.

Declining . . .

I'm afraid I can't.

Maybe some other time.

Likes/Dislikes

Inquiring about . . .

What do you like to do in your free time?

Where do you like to *run?*
What do you like to *bake?*
What kind of *books* do you like to *read?*
Which *program* do you like?
Who's your favorite *movie star?*

Expressing Likes

I like to *run*.

I like *comedies*.

Expressing Dislikes

I don't like *comedies* very much.

Intention

Inquiring about . . .

What are you going to do *this weekend?*

Expressing . . .

I'm going to *paint my apartment*.

Obligation

Expressing . . .

I have to *work late*.

Advice-Suggestions

Offering . . .

Let's *go to the beach*.

Ability/Inability

Expressing Inability

I'm afraid I can't.

Disappointment

That's too bad.

Leave Taking

Have a good weekend!
You, too.

Satisfaction/Dissatisfaction

Inquiring about . . .

Did you enjoy it?

Expressing Satisfaction

Yes. It was excellent.

Conversation Strategy

Checking and Indicating Understanding

Checking One's Own Understanding

Tonight?

TOPIC VOCABULARY GLOSSARY

The number after each word indicates the page where the word first appears.

(n) = noun
(v) = verb

Clothing

belt 63
blouse 62
boots 66
coat 62
dress 62
earrings 66
gloves 64
jacket 64
jeans 67
necklace 66
pajamas 67
pants 62
purse 67
raincoat 63
shirt 62
shoes 62
skirt 64
sneakers 64
stockings 66
sweater 63
tie (n) 62
umbrella 62
watch (n) 66

Colors

black 63
brown 63
gray 63
green 63
yellow 63

Community

bank 12
bus station 18
clinic 12
department store 22
drug store 18
gas station 19
grocery store 19
hospital 19
hotel 19
laundromat 12
library 12
mall 13
movies (movie theater) 13
museum 13
park (n) 12
parking lot 19
police station 19
post office 12
school 13
shopping mall 23
supermarket 12
theater 24
train station 23

Countries

Egypt 6
Italy 6
Japan 6
Mexico 6
The Soviet Union 6

Days of the Week 41

Sunday
Monday
Tuesday
Wednesday
Thursday
Friday
Saturday

Department Store

aisle 62
bedroom furniture 65
camera 66
counter 62
dressing room 65
elevator 65
fan 67
price 66
rack 62
radio 65
receipt 67
refrigerator 65
rest rooms 65
sale 66
TV 65
videogame 67

Describing

big 64
easy 67
heavy 67
large 64
long 64
noisy 67
short 64
small 63
tight 64

Describing People

height
- very tall 73
- tall 73
- short 73
- very short 73

weight
- thin 73
- heavy 73

hair
- blond/blonde 73
- brown 73
- curly 73
- dark 73
- gray 73

Emergencies

ambulance 57
emergency 57
fire department 57
hospital 57
police 57
police emergency unit 57

Employment

Getting a Job

ad 41
application form 40
employed 44
experienced 42
hobbies 47
hours 46
interview 41
job 40
position 44
salary 46
skills 42
special interests 47
work schedule 46

Job Procedures & Skills

act 42
clean *rooms* 40
clean *the aisles* 45
clean *the supply room* 78
close *the drawer* 76
dance 42
dial *the other office* 75
do *lab tests* 42
drive *a truck* 41
file 42
fill out *this timesheet* 75
fix *cars* 40
flip *this switch* 74
hang up 75
help *customers* 45
inspect *the car* 79
light *this oven* 75
list *your hours* 75
lock *the cash register* 76
make *beds* 40
make *eggs and sandwiches* 40
make *salads* 43
make *the beds* 78
open *this door* 74
operate *a forklift* 43
operate *a heating system* 42
operate *kitchen equipment* 40
operate *office equipment* 41
operate *the freight elevator* 75
operate *X-ray equipment* 42
paint 78
place *the paper on the glass* 77
press *this button* 74
pull *this chain* 74
punch in 74
push *this button* 74
put *a match in the hole* 75
put down *the cover* 77
put in *your time card* 74
repair *the TV* 79
repair *things* 42
repair *vacuum cleaners and toasters* 43
serve *the food* 45
set *the amount* 75
sign *at the bottom* 75
sing 42
spray *the wax* 77
start *this dishwasher* 74
stock *the shelves* 45
sweep *the floor* 81
take *blood* 42
take *inventory* 42
take *orders* 45
take out *your tray* 76
take *shorthand* 42
talk *with customers* 42
teach *Biology* 41
transfer *a call* 75
turn off *this light* 74
turn on *the gas* 75
turn *the key* 76
type 41
type *the letters* 79
use *a cash register* 40
use *a copying machine* 43
use *cleaning equipment* 42
use *laboratory equipment* 41
use *the postage machine* 75
use *word-processing equipment* 43
wash *the glasses* 78

Objects on the Job

cash register 76
copying machine 77
floor 73
forklift 78
freight elevator 75
key 73
locker 80
machine 74
postage machine 75
soda machine 72
time card 74
timesheet 75

Occupations

actor 42
cashier 40
cook (n) 40
custodian 42
dishwasher 40
driver 41
ESL teacher 44
housekeeper 40
lab technician 41
mechanic 40
medical technician 42
movie star 92
office assistant 41
player 93
sales clerk 42
salesperson 44
science teacher 41
secretary 41
security guard 44
singer 93
stock clerk 45
TV star 93
typist 44

IRREGULAR VERBS

be	was/were
bleed	bled
break	broke
buy	bought
catch	caught
come	came
cut	cut
do	did
drive	drove
eat	ate
fall	fell
feed	fed
feel	felt
find	found
fit	fit
forget	forgot
get	got
give	gave
go	went
hang	hung
have	had
hear	heard
hit	hit
hold	held
hurt	hurt
keep	kept
know	knew
lay	laid
leave	left
lend	lent
lie	lay

lose	lost
make	made
mean	meant
meet	met
overhear	overheard
pay	paid
put	put
quit	quit
read	read
ride	rode
ring	rang
run	ran
say	said
see	saw
send	sent
set	set
sit	sat
speak	spoke
stand	stood
steal	stole
sweep	swept
swim	swam
take	took
teach	taught
tell	told
think	thought
throw	threw
understand	understood
wear	wore
write	wrote

INDEX OF FUNCTIONS AND CONVERSATION STRATEGIES

INDEX OF TOPICS

INDEX OF GRAMMATICAL STRUCTURES